DOMINOES

Studio Five

LEVEL ONE   400 HEADWORDS

OXFORD
UNIVERSITY PRESS

Great Clarendon Street, Oxford OX2 6DP

Oxford University Press is a department of the University of Oxford.
It furthers the University's objective of excellence in research, scholarship,
and education by publishing worldwide in

Oxford New York

Auckland Cape Town Dar es Salaam Hong Kong Karachi
Kuala Lumpur Madrid Melbourne Mexico City Nairobi
New Delhi Shanghai Taipei Toronto

With offices in

Argentina Austria Brazil Chile Czech Republic France Greece
Guatemala Hungary Italy Japan Poland Portugal Singapore
South Korea Switzerland Thailand Turkey Ukraine Vietnam

OXFORD and OXFORD ENGLISH are registered trade marks of
Oxford University Press in the UK and in certain other countries

ISBN: 978 0 19 424765 8 BOOK
ISBN: 978 0 19 424729 0 BOOK AND MULTIROM PACK
MULTIROM NOT AVAILABLE SEPARATELY

ACKNOWLEDGEMENTS

Illustrations by: James Wetherall/Jelly (cover and story illustrations); Dylan Teague p 42
(underground map)

DOMINOES

Series Editors: Bill Bowler and Sue Parminter

Studio Five

Anthony Manning

Illustrated by James Wetherall

Anthony Manning is a keen language learner and he has lived and worked as a teacher in China, Japan, France and Germany. He was born in the Isle of Man, but now lives in the south of England where he works as a university tutor. When he is not teaching or writing he enjoys studying linguistics, travelling, cooking and socializing with friends. This is his first book for Dominoes.

OXFORD
UNIVERSITY PRESS

BEFORE READING

1 **Fay Friend works on** *The Friends' Hour* **radio show. Here are some more people in the story** *Studio Five.* **Who are they? Match the sentences with the pictures.**

Fay Friend

a **Jason Hill** is Fay's boss at Sun Radio. He isn't very nice to her.

b Young **Simon Jones** calls Fay, and speaks to her on *The Friends' Hour*.

c **Margaret Jones** is Simon's mother. She calls Sun Radio and wants to speak to Fay.

d **Wing Cheung** works with Fay on *The Friends' Hour* and is her friend.

2 **Who says this in Chapter 1?**

a I left home ten months ago.

b *The Friends' Hour* isn't interesting.

c Fay, there's one more call for you.

d What does Jason want now?

e I heard Simon on the show and I want Fay's help.

Chapter 1 • Two callers and a photo

'Four-three-two-one, **on air**.' I hear this every day before my **show** begins. Usually I'm in **Studio** Five. I make my show there.

Music plays and then I say, 'My name's Fay Friend and this is *The Friends' Hour*.' My show is on Sun Radio. It's on three times a week, Wednesday, Thursday and Saturday. A lot of the time I'm in Studio Five. I play the music and talk in between it. I love talking to the people on my show. Sometimes they want music. Sometimes they want to talk to someone.

When I'm not in Studio Five, I'm in my office. I was in my office one Thursday morning in November when I got an **email** from my **boss**. His name's Jason Hill. His office is next to my office. Jason doesn't like talking. He likes email.

'*The Friends' Hour* isn't interesting,' he wrote in his email to me. 'Nobody's listening to the show. You need to find something new. You need to think of something soon! I want to meet you next Monday for a talk.' I was very angry. The show was good, I thought. But I had four days to think of something new. Two months ago Jason was my friend. Now he's always angry with me.

on air when people can hear you on their radios

show you watch or listen to this on TV or radio

studio a room where people make TV or radio shows

music people listen or dance to this

email words that you send from computer to computer

boss the person that you work for

'This is The Friends' Hour'

1

My show begins at 11.00 in the morning. It finishes at 12.00. The weather comes after it. The time was 11.55. I put on some music. Then I called Wing. Wing Cheung works with me. He answers the phone. He also helps me to make the show. Wing is a big help. My mother died in May. Wing **really** helped me then too. I was very sad about mum. I didn't eat, I didn't talk and I didn't work for days after she died. Wing was nice to me about mum. He helped me at work, too. He's a very good friend.

'Wing, are there any more phone calls?'

'Fay, there's one more call for you. But make it quick.' Wing always watches the time. I always forget.

'OK,' I said. 'Is it an easy call?'

'No, it isn't.' The music finished. The next caller waited.

'There's time for one more call before the show finishes,' I said. 'Caller, what's your name? Where are you from?' After a second, the caller spoke.

'Hi Fay, Erm ... I'm Simon, Simon Jones. This is for my mother. She likes your show, I know. I-I left home six months ago. I don't want to see her, but I'm fine ... I'm well, I mean. I'm not far away, but I'm not coming home. I must go now.' Simon was angry and very **sad**. Families aren't always easy, I thought. My mother and my father were dead. I felt sad about that.

'Simon, are you there? Hello?' I said, but Simon wasn't on the phone now. I finished the show with some more music. The weather began at 12.00.

After the show, I thought about Simon Jones again. He wasn't happy at all. In the afternoon I worked on the show for the next day. I didn't understand Jason. *The Friends' Hour* was good, I thought, but he didn't like it. What did

really truly
sad not happy

2

he want? What could I do to please him? I didn't know. I drank a lot of coffee. Nothing came to me. At 4.00 Wing ran into my office.

'Wing! I'm working.' I was angry again. I thought about Jason's email.

'Sorry, Fay, but I had a call about today's show.'

'Was it Jason again? What does he want now?'

At 4.00 Wing ran into my office.

'No it wasn't Jason. It was a woman. Margaret Jones is her name. She's Simon's mother.'

'What does she want?' I asked.

'She wants your help, I think,' said Wing. 'She gave me her home phone number, and her house number, and the street ...'

'Look Wing, how can I help her?' I said angrily. Wing went back to his office.

Then I thought about my mother and father again. My father died fourteen years ago. I was eleven at the time. He was a **police officer**. My mother always wanted me to be a police officer too. But I wanted to work for the radio. When I began working for Sun Radio, Mum and I didn't speak for two years. Then she died. That was six months ago. I felt really bad because we didn't talk. But perhaps I could help Mrs Jones ...?

But no, I really had no time for that. I had only four days to think of something new for my show. I **tried** to work again. After five minutes I looked at my computer. There was one more angry email on it from Jason. That was it! I went to Wing's office.

'Where does the Jones family live?' I asked. He told me the name of the street and the house number. I left Sun Radio and ran to the **underground station**. I needed to talk to Mrs Jones.

At 5.15 I was at Piccadilly Circus. Piccadilly Circus is the nearest station to Sun Radio. Margaret Jones's house was near Finchley Road station. After about twenty minutes I arrived at Finchley Road.

I left the station and ran past all the people in the street. No time to smile. No time to talk. I thought about Simon. 'Where is he? Why is he unhappy?'

I walked past a supermarket, coffee shops, and some offices. After five minutes I arrived at South Road. Mrs Jones lived at number twenty-six. South Road was a street with lots of big red houses on it, and one little shop – number twenty. I saw the name – 'Khan's One Stop Shop' – over the door.

police officer a man or a woman who stops people doing bad things

try to want to do something but not to do it well

underground a train that goes under streets and buildings

station people get on and off trains here

Suddenly I felt thirsty. It was all that coffee earlier in the studio! I needed some water. I went into the shop. It had many different things in it: things to read, things to eat and things to drink. I found some water, and I gave the money to the man in the shop. Then I walked to the door. There I stopped. I saw something on the back of the door. It was a photo of a young man. Under the photo I read, 'Where is Simon Jones?' And under that question there was a phone number to call. I had lots of questions about Simon, and I needed some answers fast. Perhaps the man in the shop could help me?

I arrived at South Road.

READING CHECK

Complete the sentences with the correct names.

Wing   Jason   Fay   Simon

a .....Wing..... is Fay's good friend.

b .... is angry with Fay.

c Fay works with .... and .... in Studio Five.

d .... likes emails, not talking to people.

e .... calls Fay's show after 10 months away from home.

f ....'s father was a police officer.

g ....'s mother and father are dead.

h .... doesn't want to go home.

i .... helped Fay when she felt very bad in May.

WORD WORK

1 Use the words in the coffee cup to complete these sentences.

a I want to be a .police officer... when I leave school.

b 'Can you speak Arabic?'
'Not very well, but I'm .... to learn it.'

c 'Are we .... now?'
'Yes, we are. So what do you want to say to all our listeners?'

d Paddington is one of the bigger and more important train .... in London.

ACTIVITIES

e To get from A to B in London, go by .... There's not much to see down there, but it's very quick.

f We felt very .... when our daughter left home.

2 Use words from Chapter 1 to complete Jason's second email to Fay.

From: jasonhill@sunradio.com   Sent: Thursday 10 November

To: fayfriend@sunradio.com   Subject: Me Again!

Dear Fay,

A new a)..... *email* .... from me. We must talk about your b)................. on Monday morning. Shakira! James Blunt! It's c)................. boring listening to d).............. .. all the time.

e) .... Five needs something more interesting than this!

From your f)................. ,
Jason

GUESS WHAT

What do we learn about Simon in the next chapter? Tick four boxes.

a He worked in Khan's One-Stop Shop. ☐

b He helped his mother a lot when she went through bad times. ☐

c He's in love with a beautiful young woman from Pakistan. ☐

d He was angry with his mother before he left home. ☐

e He loves everything about trains. ☐

f He's visiting Europe by train now. ☐

Chapter 2 • A card and a train

'Are you Mr Khan?' I asked the man in the shop.

'Yes, I am,' he said.

'Do you know the man in this photo?'

'Yes, I do. He lived in South Road. He worked here for two years. He was a good worker.'

'When did he leave?'

*'Are you
Mr Khan?'*

'Erm … in January, I think,' said Mr Khan. 'I told Simon, "You must move to a different shop now." I have six shops in London, and I need good workers in all of them, you see. But Simon said "no". He wanted to work near home because he needed the money. He loved trains, you know. He wanted to visit Europe by train. I didn't see him often after that. But I told the police everything about Simon months ago. Who are you?'

'I'm Simon's friend,' I said.

'So why did he leave? Do you know?'

8

'No, I don't. He was always very friendly, always laughed a lot. Then suddenly everything changed. He was different – sadder. Perhaps something happened at home, I don't know. He was very quiet. Simon's house is near here. Number twenty-six South Road. Go and talk to his mother. She's a nice woman. She put up that photo in my shop. Simon was very good to her after his father died. He's a good boy.'

'When did Mr Jones die?' I asked.

'Three years ago, I think. Are you really Simon's friend? You don't know him very well,' Mr Khan said.

I thanked him and walked to the door again. Mr Khan went to the back of the shop and made a telephone call. He couldn't see me. I took the photo of Simon from the back of the door and put it in my bag. Then I went quickly to twenty-six South Road. I needed to talk to Mrs Jones.

A woman opened the front door. She had grey hair.

'Hi, I'm Fay Friend,' I said. 'I work for Sun Radio. You telephoned my studio this afternoon. Can we talk about Simon?'

'You came. That's wonderful. Thank you. Please come in.' Mrs Jones took me to the living room. She made tea and sat down next to me.

'On the phone you asked for my help,' I said.

'That's right.' Mrs Jones put her head in her hands. She was very sad.

'I must find Simon,' she said.

'What can I do? I'm not a detective,' I thought.

'You can help me, I know. Please say "yes" Fay,' she cried. I thought of my family again. I really wanted to help her.

'OK,' I said. I took Mrs Jones's hand. 'Tell me everything. Why did Simon leave?'

Mrs Jones looked up into my eyes and told me her story.

'Our family was happy for many years. Then my husband, Peter, died. It was a bad time for Simon and for me. I was very sad. But Simon really helped me when everything was black. Then something **terrible** happened ...' Mrs Jones cried again.

'What?' I asked.

'Ten months ago Simon found some old letters. They were from my old boyfriend, Geoff. My husband, Peter, wasn't Simon's **real** father, you see. Geoff was Simon's father but he left me only a month or two before Simon was born. He didn't want children. Then I met Peter. He was very good to me and we **fell in love**. Soon after that, Peter **married** me. He was a good husband and a good father to Simon. But Simon never knew the true story. After he found Geoff's letters, he was very angry with me. We didn't talk for two days. Then Simon left home. That was ten months ago now. Where is he now? I have no **idea**. But I can't live without him!'

I looked at Mrs Jones, and thought of my mother.

'I'm going to help you,' I said. But what could I do? My father was a police officer, but I work on a radio show. I didn't have any answers, but I knew Mrs Jones needed me.

'Thank you very much, Fay. Now look at this. Two months ago, on the 21st of September, I was fifty. I got this **card** on my **birthday**.' Mrs Jones gave a card in an **envelope** to me. There was a picture of red flowers on the card. I opened it and read it:

Dear Mum, I'm fine. Don't **worry**! love, Simon

terrible very bad

real true

fall in love (past **fell**) to begin to love someone

marry to make someone your husband or wife

idea something that you think

card something that you send someone on their birthday

birthday the day when someone was born

envelope a paper cover that you put in a letter

worry to be unhappy about something and to think about it all the time

Now I had the phone call, the photo from Mr Khan's shop, and the card to help me. But I needed to understand Simon better.

'Mrs Jones, can I see Simon's room before I go?' I asked.

'Yes, of course. I didn't move a thing when he left.'

Mrs Jones took me upstairs and opened the door of Simon's bedroom. I wanted to learn more about him. The room was very **tidy** – with a bed, a table, a chair and a computer in it. On the table I found some train tickets and a **model** train. I remembered my talk with Ahmed Khan. Simon loved trains. I looked at the computer, and I read Simon's emails – but they didn't help. What could I do next? I didn't know. I thanked Mrs Jones and left South Road. I needed to think. I went back to the Sun Radio building.

tidy with everything carefully where it is right to be

model little buildings, trains, cars, ships or planes that children make and then play with

Simon loved trains.

READING CHECK

Correct the mistakes in these sentences.

a ~~Jason~~ *Simon* worked with Mr Khan in the past.

b Mr Khan has one shop in London.

c Mr Khan put up the photo of Simon in the shop.

d Simon found letters from Mrs Jones's old teacher.

e Peter was Simon's true father.

f Simon felt happy when he learned about Geoff.

g Simon left home long after that.

h Mrs Jones got a card from Geoff on her 50th birthday.

i Fay finds some plane tickets on the table in Simon's room.

WORD WORK

Use the words from the train in the correct form to complete the sentences on page 13.

idea terrible worry real tidy envelope card model fall in love marry birthday

ACTIVITIES

a He really can't play the guitar and he's a ..terrible.. singer, too.

b Do you like my new .... of 'The Titanic'? I made it yesterday.

c She isn't my .... sister. She's the daughter of my mother's second husband.

d Their room isn't very .... They leave their things everywhere.

e I'd like a 'Get Well' .... for my grandmother, please. She's ill in hospital.

f He'll be eighteen next month. It's his .... on the twelfth.

g What a good ....! Let's go to the cinema.

h She took the letter from her boyfriend out of its .... and read it quickly.

i Many mothers and fathers .... when their children come home late.

j I met my girlfriend last year in Italy and we ....
.... at once.

k Jane looked beautiful in her white dress when she .... Frank in the village church on Saturday.

GUESS WHAT

What happens in the next chapter? Tick the boxes.

1 Wing . . .

a . . . goes for a walk with Simon. ☐

b . . . opens the Sun Radio door again for Fay. ☐

c . . . smokes a cigarette with Jason. ☐

2 Fay . . .

a . . . writes a letter to Mrs Jones. ☐

b . . . has dinner with Wing. ☐

c . . . takes something from Jason's office. ☐

3 Jason . . .

a . . . asks Fay out for dinner. ☐

b . . . speaks to Simon. ☐

c . . . gives Fay more time to find new ideas for her show. ☐

Chapter 3 • Can the CD help?

I arrived back at Sun Radio at 6.30. I opened my bag but I couldn't find my **keys** in it. So I found my phone and called Wing. It was late but perhaps he was at work.

'Hello, Studio Five. Wing Cheung here,' Wing answered.

'Wonderful! You're there,' I said.

'You forgot your keys again, Fay. So I waited for you.'

'Thanks, Wing. Can you let me in?' Wing opened the door for me. I went up to my office in Studio Five and sat down.

'Thanks for waiting. I'm sorry about the keys,' I said, and smiled at Wing. 'He's a true friend,' I thought. Sometimes I thought about Wing and me. I didn't have a boyfriend, and I really liked being with Wing. I didn't tell him all that, of course. I didn't want to lose a good friend.

'I've got some bad news, Fay,' said Wing. 'You've got one more email from the boss. Jason isn't happy with today's show.'

Suddenly the phone in my office rang. It was Jason. I felt ill. I was back in Sun Radio, and he knew it. He wanted to talk to me. I walked slowly to his office.

'Good evening. Nice to have you back with us,' he said. He had a smile on his face but he was angry, I knew. 'Do you remember my email this morning?' he asked.

'Yes, of course,' I said. 'You want new ideas for the show. I'm working on it.'

'Fay, this is important. No ideas – no show, and no show – no **job**. Think about it! I listened to today's show. You really have a lot of work to do.' I saw the **CD** of today's show on his **desk**.

key you can close or open a door with this

job work

CD people listen to music on this

desk a table in a study or in an office

'I'm going to finish working on some new ideas tomorrow,' I said.

'Perhaps you want to move to Studio Ten?' he laughed. The people in Studio Ten make early morning shows. 'In Studio Ten, they get up at four in the morning every day, you know.' Jason didn't like Studio Ten because he didn't like early mornings.

Jason opened the window. He had a cigarette in his hand. He sat back in his chair and smoked. His feet were on the desk.

'Do you need more time, Fay?' he asked.

'Of course I need more time,' I said. 'I've got only three days.'

'So have dinner with me tonight. Let's have a nice evening out. Then I can easily give you more time. I like you, Fay. You know that.'

'Oh, now I see,' I said. 'Well, the answer is "no"! I don't need more time. Monday is OK for me. And now, excuse me. I'm going.' I ran out of Jason's office, closed the door behind me, and then I cried. I couldn't stop. I walked back into Studio Five, but Wing saw my face.

He sat back in his chair and smoked.

'What's the matter, Fay?' Wing put his hand on my arm.

'Jason's really angry with me,' I said. 'I need to do a lot of work on the show before Monday.' Then I told Wing about my visit to South Road.

'You feel bad about your mum, Fay. But you can't really help Mrs Jones. You're not a detective. And what about the show?' said Wing.

He took my hand in his hand. 'I need –' he began. Then his face was suddenly red.

'What?' I asked.

'Oh, it's nothing,' he said, and he moved away.

'Wing, Mrs Jones needs help,' I said, 'And I need to help her. I'm sorry, but I'm going to think about the show tomorrow.'

'OK!' said Wing. 'But you can't do all this detective work **alone**. I can help you.'

'Thank you,' I said quietly.

'So let's think,' said Wing. 'Simon left in January. Then he sent a card to his mum in September. Is that right?'

'Yes. And he likes trains, too.'

'Right. Let's listen to today's show again,' said Wing. 'Perhaps we didn't hear something important in Simon's call.'

'The CD's in Jason's office,' I said. We went to Jason's office. But he wasn't there, and the door was **locked**.

'It's no good. We can't get in,' said Wing. 'Perhaps tomorrow–'

'This can't wait!' I said. Then I had an idea. I ran back to my office, and I took off my shoes. Then I stood on my desk and opened my office window.

Wing came after me.

alone with nobody

locked closed with a key

16

'What are you doing?' he asked.

'Jason's office window is open. I can **climb** out here and get into his office through the open window.'

'What?! It's not **safe**. We're five **floors** up!'

'Don't worry,' I said. I put my head out of the window. Then I climbed out and stood on the window **ledge**. It was very cold out there. I looked down. I saw cars far down in the street. They were no bigger than model cars. I didn't look down again. I didn't want to **fall**. Then I thought of Simon and of my family. Suddenly I moved quickly along the ledge.

'Be careful!' said Wing. I nearly fell through the window into Jason's office. There I took the CD from his desk and opened the office door. Wing was happy to see me back safely.

'Fay,' he said. 'You're **crazy**!'

'I know,' I said. I felt really excited. We went into Studio Five, and we listened to Simon's call very carefully.

I moved along the ledge

climb to go up, down, or through something using your hands and feet

safe in no danger

floor the place in a room where you stand and walk.

ledge a long flat stone under a window

fall (past **fell**) to go down suddenly

crazy not thinking well

READING CHECK

Choose the correct words to complete these sentences.

a Wing/Fay forgets his/her keys.

b Jason/Wing opens the door for Fay.

c Jason likes/doesn't like Studio Ten.

d Jason/Wing asks Fay out for dinner.

e Fay really wants/doesn't want to go out with him.

f Jason/Wing helps Fay with her detective work.

g Wing/Fay gets into Jason's office through the window.

WORD WORK

1 Find ten more words from Chapter 3 in the CD.

2 Use the words from Activity 1 to complete the sentences.

a Fay likes her ......*job*...... at Studio Five a lot. She loves working there.

b She can't find her ...., so Wing must open the door for her.

c She can't find Simon ...., but Wing can work with her and help her.

d The .... of today's show is in Jason's office, on his ....

e Jason is going home, and the door to his office is ....

f First Fay .... out of her window.

g 'That's not .... ,' says Wing. 'Be careful!'

h Studio Five is on the fifth .... of the Sun Radio building.

i Then Fay stands on the window .... and looks down.

j She doesn't want to .... down to the street.

k 'You're .... ,' says Wing when Fay comes back through the window.

GUESS WHAT

What happens to Fay in the next chapter? Tick three boxes.

a She goes to Paddington station. ☐

b She loses her bag. ☐

c She finds Simon. ☐

d She meets an old friend. ☐

e She goes to a card shop. ☐

f She falls under a train. ☐

Chapter 4 • The card shop at the station

'Wing, it's no good,' I said. 'I don't want to listen to that CD again. Not after five times. There's nothing there. I must tell Mrs Jones tomorrow. I can't help her any more.'

'Wait!' said Wing, 'I've got an idea. We're listening to the wrong things. We need to listen one more time. But I need the computer for that.' So he played the CD on the computer. This time we heard different noises in the **background**. These noises were very quiet before. But on the computer we could hear them easily. First we heard people's **voices** in the background. Then we heard the **sound** of **coins**.

'Perhaps Simon called us from a phone box,' said Wing.

'That doesn't help us much. How many phone boxes are there in London?' I said.

'Shh! Listen to this,' said Wing. Now we heard a new voice in the background.

'This is a **platform** change. The 11.45 to Oxford is now leaving from platform 6.'

'Simon was at a train station!' said Wing. He was very happy.

'You're right,' I said. 'And it was a train to Oxford. Perhaps it's a London station!'

I looked on the **Internet**. Trains to Oxford leave London from Paddington Station. Then I had an idea. I took Mrs Jones's card from my bag and looked carefully at the envelope. The **postcode** on the **date stamp** was W2 25. I looked on the Internet again. Simon sent the card from Paddington Station! The name of a shop was on the back of the card, too. It was Cards 4U. I knew that name. There

background something that is under the most important noise on a CD or behind the most important thing in a picture

voice you use this to speak

sound noise

coin metal money

platform you get on a train in a station from this

Internet you use a computer and a phone line to find different things on this

postcode you write these numbers and letters on an envelope under the city

date stamp this mark on an envelope shows a postman when and from where someone sent a letter

was a Cards 4U shop in Piccadilly Circus underground station.

'Perhaps there's a shop at Paddington, too,' I thought. 'And perhaps Simon works there.' I took the card and the photo of Simon and I put them in my bag.

'I'm going to find Simon,' I told Wing. 'He's at Paddington, I think.'

'Good luck, Fay!' said Wing with a smile. 'Don't worry about me,' he said. 'I'm going to wait here and think about changes to your show. Don't forget you're meeting Jason on Monday.'

I arrived at Paddington underground station at about 9.30. I walked up to the train station. I saw some small shops near to the trains. Then I saw the name 'Cards 4U' over one shop window. I went quickly into the shop.

'Can I help you?' said the woman in the shop. It was late and nearly time for her to close.

'I'm not sure,' I said. 'I don't need a card. I'm looking for a friend. He works here, I think. His name's Simon.'

'There's no Simon here,' she said.

*'There's no
Simon here.'*

I put my bag on a table and took out the photo from Mr Khan's shop.

'My name's Fay Friend,' I said. 'Do you know this man?' I asked.

'No,' said the woman. 'He doesn't work here.'

So I was wrong.

'I'm sorry, Miss. I'm going to close now,' said the woman.

Suddenly I saw a young man in the station. He walked past the card shop. 'It's Simon!' I thought. I took the photo and ran after him. Then I got nearer to the man. It wasn't Simon. I was wrong again.

I walked away from the card shop. I didn't understand. Simon called me from Paddington Station. He bought the card from Cards 4U. But where was he? I had no idea.

For the next thirty minutes I talked to different people in the station.

'Do you know this man?' I asked. People looked at the photo. But nobody knew Simon. After thirty minutes I needed a coffee, so I went to the coffee shop in the station. I asked for a big coffee with milk.

'That's one pound seventy-five,' said the man in the coffee shop.

'Oh no!' I said. 'My bag! I left it in the card shop.'

'My bag! I left it in the card shop.'

I ran out without my coffee. Quickly I put my hand in my coat pocket. I had only the photo, my phone and my train ticket there. My keys, my money, the card – they were all in my bag. This was very bad.

I ran to the card shop. I was hot and tired when I arrived. But the shop was closed. Then I saw the woman from the shop not far away from me in the station. I ran after her.

'Excuse me, do you have my bag? I left it in your shop, I think.'

'Don't worry,' she said. 'Your bag's safe. I left it at the **Lost Property Office**.'

For a minute I was happy. Then I looked at my watch. It was five past ten.

'What time does the Lost Property Office close?' I asked.

'Ten o'clock,' the woman said. 'I'm sorry. You're five minutes late. But it's OK. I told them your name. And the office opens again at nine o'clock tomorrow. Don't worry.'

I thanked the woman, but I wasn't happy. I had no money, and no keys to Sun Radio, or to my house. I felt bad about Simon, bad about the show, bad about my bag, bad about everything. How could I lose my keys **twice** in one day? What a terrible day! I took my train ticket from my pocket and went back to Sun Radio.

Lost Property Office people can find things they lose or forget here

twice two times

I wasn't happy.

READING CHECK

What do they say?

a 'I don't want to listen to that CD again,'

b 'Simon was at a train station!'

c 'I'm looking for a friend,'

d 'I'm sorry, Miss. I must close now,'

e 'That's one pound seventy-five,'

f 'Oh no! My bag!'

g 'Don't worry. It's safe,'

1 says the man in the coffee shop to Fay.

2 says the woman from the shop to Fay in the station.

3 says the woman to Fay in the card shop.

4 says Wing to Fay.

5 says Fay to the man in the coffee shop.

6 says Fay to the woman in the card shop.

7 says Fay to Wing.

WORD WORK

1 **Find words in Chapter 4 to complete the puzzle.**

Across

3 A euro is one of these.

4 You can get lots of answers to any questions from this through computers and phones.

6 The day someone sends a letter goes on this.

9 You use this to talk with.

Down

1 These letters and numbers in an address help the postman to find a house.

2 A different word for a 'noise'.

5 When you hear noises behind a speaker's voice on a CD, they are in the
   . . . .

7 One word for 'two times'.

8 You get off a train onto this in a station.

2 Write the coloured letters in order to find the name of an important train station in London.

∨

3 Use the words in Activity 1 in the correct form to complete the notes in Wing's notebook.

There were different noises in the a)..background.. on
the CD. We heard people's b)......................... and also the
c)........................... of d)........................... in a phone box.
We heard about a e)........................... change for a train too.
Fay looked carefully at the September f)...........................
.... on the envelope from Mrs Jones's birthday
card. She looked on the g)........................... to learn more
about different London h)........................... . The card came
from Paddington station.

GUESS WHAT

What does Fay find and lose in the next chapter? Tick three boxes.

a She finds . . .
  1 her bag. ☐
  2 love with her boss, Jason. ☐
  3 Simon Jones. ☐

b She loses . . .
  1 her job. ☐
  2 her good friend Wing for a time. ☐
  3 her train ticket. ☐

Chapter 5 • Lost Property

I went back to Piccadilly Circus. It was 10.35 in the evening.

'Please be at work in Studio Five, Wing,' I thought. 'Then you can open the door for me again, and I can sleep on the floor in my office.'

I called Wing, but he didn't answer. Then I saw a light in Jason's office. I called his number. I didn't want to call him, but I needed help.

'Hello. Jason Hill,' he answered.

'Hi. This is Fay. Can you open the door for me?'

'Did you lose your keys again, Fay? You must be more careful,' he said.

'They're on my desk. I want to work on *the Friend's Hour* tonight,' I said. It wasn't true, but Jason opened the door for me.

'You're working late, Fay. Very good!' Jason was nicer to me now. 'He isn't a bad boss really,' I thought.

'You're working late, Fay. Very good!'

26

I went into my office. I wanted to forget about the day. I was tired, hungry, and alone. Just then, Jason came in.

'What about that dinner, Fay? Don't worry. I can **pay**. I want to thank you for all your work on the show.' I was really tired. It was all very sudden. I couldn't think. I didn't want to be in the office, and Jason was really friendly.

'OK,' I said. 'We were good friends before,' I thought. I got my coat and put some office keys in my pocket. I needed to come back there later.

We went to a little Italian restaurant near Sun Radio. We ate well, and we drank a bottle of red **wine**. It was a nice evening, but it didn't feel right. 'Why is Jason doing this?' I thought. At 11.30 it was time to leave. Jason paid and we went to the door. Suddenly everything changed. He tried to **kiss** me.

'Stop it!' I told him.

'Fay, take it easy! I can help you,' he said. And he put his hand on my leg.

'Take your hands off me! You're crazy. I don't need your help!' I cried. I ran back to Sun Radio. Jason didn't run after me. It began to rain. I felt worse than before.

At 8.30 the next morning I woke up in the office. I thought about the show again. I was tired and I had no ideas. It was Friday and I didn't have much time. I needed to get my bag from Paddington Station. I opened my office door and saw Jason in front of me.

'Fay, you look bad,' he said. My hair was terrible. My face was tired. 'Where are you going?' he asked.

'Out,' I said. Just then Wing arrived.

'Good morning. Terrible weather again,' said Wing.

pay (*past* **paid**) to give money for something

wine a red or white drink; when you drink a lot you feel happy and sleepy

kiss to touch lovingly with your mouth

'Fay, you must tell Wing about our wonderful evening yesterday,' said Jason. 'We had a very nice bottle of wine between the two of us.' He smiled and then went into his office.

Wing didn't say a word. But he looked at me, and his eyes were big and sad.

'You've got the wrong idea, Wing,' I said. I didn't love Jason. But I didn't have time to tell Wing that. I needed to go back to Paddington Station.

I got to the Lost Property Office there at about 9.10.

'Can I help you?' asked the man there. I told him about my bag and he asked me some questions. 'When did you lose it? Where? What colour was it? What was in it?' I answered them all.

'OK, Miss. Let's see.' He went into the back of the office and looked around. Then a young man brought my bag out to me. I looked at the photo of Simon again. 'Is this young man Simon?' I thought. But his hair was longer and it was a different colour. Slowly I walked away from the office and put the photo in my bag. Suddenly I saw something new in my bag. It was a **note**. It wasn't there when I left the bag in the card shop. It said:

> Meet me in the coffee shop at 10 o'clock. We need to talk.

I looked at my watch. It was only 9.30. I spoke to some more people in the station. Again, they looked at the photo of Simon, but nobody knew him. I wanted to cry. I tried to call Wing, but he didn't answer.

note a short letter

At 10 o'clock I went to the coffee shop. The man there smiled at me. He remembered me from the night before. I paid for a coffee and sat in a chair near the door 'Who put that note in my bag?' I thought. 'Perhaps they know something about Simon.' I waited for ten minutes, but nobody came. I finished my coffee. I was ready to go. Then a young man came into the shop. It was the young man from the Lost Property Office.

'Are you Fay Friend?' he asked.

'Yes,' I answered.

'Can I sit down?'

'Of course,' I said. I looked carefully at him again, and suddenly I took the photo of Simon from my bag. His hair was different. It was longer, and it was a different colour. But the face in the photo and the young man's face were **the same**. I couldn't stop looking at the young man in front of me. I couldn't **believe** it. It was Simon Jones!

the same not different

believe to think that something is true

'Are you Fay Friend?'

READING CHECK

Put these sentences in the correct order. Number them 1–10.

a Jason opens the door for Fay. ☐

b Fay goes back to Sun Radio. ☐ 1

c Jason asks Fay out for dinner. ☐

d Jason pays for dinner. ☐

e Fay feels alone and hungry. ☐

f Jason tries to kiss Fay. ☐

g Fay and Jason go to an Italian restaurant. ☐

h Simon Jones comes to speak to Fay. ☐

i Fay runs back to Sun Radio. ☐

j Fay gets back her bag. ☐

WORD WORK

Use the words in the spaghetti to complete the sentences on page 31.

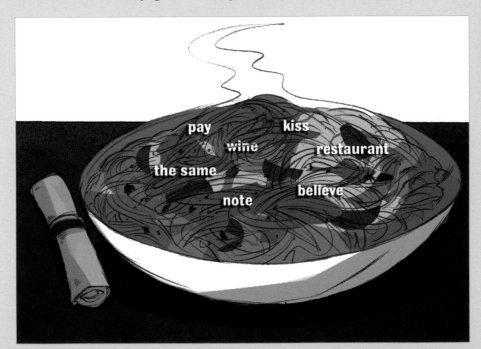

a We drank a bottle of good, old, Hungarian red ....wine........ .

b I'm feeling rich. I can .... for our dinner.

c My brother and I look .... The two of us have dark hair and green eyes.

d Move your mouth away from my face. I'm not going to .... you!

e There was a .... for me on the door and I read it.

f There's a very nice Polish .... near our house. We can eat very well there.

g It's not true! I don't .... in Father Christmas.

GUESS WHAT

What happens in the next chapter? Tick five boxes.

a Simon Jones meets his mother. ☐

b Simon goes to Australia. ☐

c *The Friends' Hour* is better than before. ☐

d Fay loses her job. ☐

e Wing stops working on *The Friends' Hour*. ☐

f Jason leaves Studio Five. ☐

g Fay finds a boyfriend – Simon! ☐

h Wing and Fay fall in love. ☐

Chapter 6 • Time to talk

flat a number of rooms in a house where someone lives

promise when you say that you will certainly do something

'Simon, is it really you?' I asked.

'Yes, Fay. I put the note in your bag. I work in the Lost Property Office. But why are you looking for me?'

'It's a long story,' I said. We talked for the next thirty minutes.

We talked for the next thirty minutes.

'Look, I'm twenty-five years old,' said Simon. 'I'm not a child. Why didn't mum tell me about my real dad? I needed to leave home. I needed time to think. Do you understand?'

'Yes, and your mother understands too. But she wants you to come back home.'

'Well, I have a room in a **flat** now. Ahmed helped me to find it. I don't want to live with my mother again.'

'Is that Ahmed Khan?' I asked.

'Yes, that's right. He has lots of shops in London. Some of them have flats upstairs. Ahmed told me about your visit to his shop.'

'Yes, I met him. But he didn't tell me about your flat.'

'I know. I told him, "Please don't give people my address." Ahmed always keeps his **promises**. He's a very good friend.'

So Ahmed Khan's story wasn't all true. But he only wanted to **protect** Simon. I understood.

'You don't need to leave your flat, Simon,' I said. 'But your mother wants to see you.'

'I'm not ready to see her. Look, Fay, why are you so interested in us? This is nothing to do with you.'

'I know that,' I said. 'But your mother called me. She asked for my help. Family is important, you know. We sometimes forget it, but it's true. My mother died six months ago. I didn't talk to her for a long time before she died. And now I can never make friends with her again. You and your mother need to talk.'

'Ok, then perhaps you can help me?'

'Of course,' I said. Just then I had a good idea. I could help the Jones family and change my show at the same time. 'I'm going to do my best, but you must help me too.' I wrote Simon's telephone number in my notebook. Then I went back to the office excitedly. I had work to do. I needed to speak to Wing about Jason too.

I worked hard in Studio Five for **the rest** of the day. I saw Wing many times but we couldn't talk. Before I went home, I called Simon and then Mrs Jones. I asked Mrs Jones, 'Can you come to Sun Radio to talk on *The Friends Hour?*' I didn't tell her about Simon.

The next day was Saturday. Wing met Simon at 9.30. I met Mrs Jones at 10 o'clock.

'We're going to talk about families on today's show,' I told her. We went into Studio Five at 10.50. The show began at 11.00.

protect to keep someone safe

the rest what is left

'Four-three-two-one – on air!' I looked at Mrs Jones and smiled. The music played. 'My name's Fay Friend and this is *The Friends' Hour*. Today we're talking about families. My **guest** is Margaret Jones.'

Mrs Jones talked about Simon. Simon listened to the show in Wing's office, but Mrs Jones didn't know that. She told the listeners about her family and about Simon's real father.

'Geoff is Simon's real father but he didn't want children. He was **selfish** and he didn't want to marry me. I was **pregnant** but he wasn't interested. He went to live in Australia, and I never saw him again.'

'So what about your husband, Peter? What was he like?' I asked.

'Peter Jones was a very different man. He truly loved me and he wanted to be a good father to Simon. He married me before Simon was born. We never talked about Geoff after that. We were happy. I never found the right time to tell Simon. Then one day he found some letters from Geoff. He didn't understand, he was angry with me, and he left home.'

We talked on air for fifteen minutes. Then I asked Mrs Jones, 'Can you close your eyes for a minute?' At first she didn't understand, but then she closed them. At the same time, Simon came into Studio Five. Then Mrs Jones opened her eyes. For a second they didn't say a thing. Then, suddenly, Mrs Jones spoke.

'I'm really happy to see you, Simon.'

'It was really difficult for you Mum, and I never knew. Peter was a true father to me. He was wonderful. Why didn't you tell me?'

guest somebody that you invite to your home, a party, or to speak on a radio show

selfish thinking only about what is good for you

pregnant when a woman is waiting for a child

'I'm sorry. I wanted to tell you.
But I never found the right time.'

'It doesn't matter. We can talk
now. It was wrong of me to walk
out. I'm sorry.'

They were happy and sad at the
same time. They talked and talked. I
was really excited. I felt good about
helping the Jones family. And I felt good
about the show too. Then I remembered the
meeting with Jason on Monday. And I remembered
about Wing, too. I felt terrible again.

On Sunday I stayed in bed for a long time. I wanted to
forget about Monday. I thought about getting a new job.
But I didn't want to leave Sun Radio, Studio Five or *The
Friends' Hour*. Suddenly I understood something. I didn't
want to lose my job, but most of all I didn't want to lose
Wing. I was in love with him.

*Then Simon
came into the
studio.*

I went to work early on Monday morning. My meeting with Jason was at ten o'clock. At 9.30 Wing came into the Studio. I was ready to talk to him. I loved him, not Jason. He needed to know.

'Wing, we need to talk,' I said. 'It's about me and Jason. You don't understand.'

'Yes, I do, Fay. It's nothing to do with me. Forget it,' he said. Then he left the room. I wanted to cry. 'I must tell him the truth!' I thought. So I wrote a note for him:

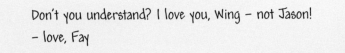

Don't you understand? I love you, Wing – not Jason!
– love, Fay

But I didn't give the note to Wing in the end. I couldn't. I felt **stupid** about it.

Suddenly I looked at my watch. It was 10 o'clock – time for my meeting! I left the note on my desk and ran to Jason's office. I **knocked** on Jason's door and waited. I felt really ill.

'Come in, Fay,' I heard, but it wasn't Jason's voice. It was a woman. I went into the room and saw two people there – Jason and his boss, Amy Jackson.

'Sit down, Fay,' said Amy. Jason said nothing. 'I'm going to lose my job,' I thought.

'Fay, the new Friends' Hour show on Saturday was truly wonderful,' said Amy. 'The listeners loved it, and we want you to do the same show – all about families and their problems – every day. You get a **pay rise** to go with your new job, too.'

Jason tried to smile, but he couldn't.

stupid not thinking well

knock to hit strongly

pay rise when the money you get for work goes up

36

'Jason's moving up to Studio Ten next month,' said Amy. 'So you can have his office on this floor. And Wing can work on a new show too. He's ready for it. Please tell him the **news**. He can see me about it this afternoon.'

news when someone tells you something that is new

hug to take lovingly in your arms

I left Jason's office. I felt happy about the show, and happy for Wing. I wanted to tell him the good news. I found him in my office – with a big smile on his face.

'Fay, Why didn't you tell me before?' he said. He **hugged** me and kissed me.'

'What do you mean?' I laughed. 'Do you know about our new jobs?'

'New jobs? No! Don't be stupid. I found your note on the desk. I read it. And I love you too, Fay.' I kissed him back.

That was a month ago. Now my new show is on air every day. The listeners love *The Friends' Hour*. Lots of interesting people call me. They're looking for lost friends and family. Things are different in Studio Five too. I don't work with Wing these days. He has a new show. I never see him at work, but it doesn't matter – because he's my boyfriend. And we're really very happy, Wing and I.

And we're really happy, Wing and I.

READING CHECK

Correct ten more mistakes in the summary of the chapter.

Fay finds Simon and tells him, 'You must talk to your ~~father~~ *mother*.'

Simon is now living in one of Ahmed Khan's shops. Fay has an idea to help the Khan family

and to make her show better too.

The next day Simon and Mr Khan meet in Studio Five. They talk on air on The Friends' Hour.

Simon learns the true story about his mother and his real sister. At the end of the show,

mother and daughter are friends again.

On Sunday, Fay has a meeting with Jason and his boss, Amy. Before the meeting, Fay writes

a card to Wing. She loves Simon, not Jason – but Wing doesn't know this. The listeners love

the new show, and Fay doesn't lose her job. Wing is going to move to Studio Ten. Fay tells

Wing about his new job and Wing tells Amy about his love for her.

WORD WORK

Use the letters in the bags to make words and complete the sentences.

a I can't go home. I have a room in a ......flat...... now. talf

b He was .... and he never thought much about me. slefshi

c I was .... but he didn't want children. grantpem

d How much was two and two? I didn't know, and I felt .... tipsud

e My brother and I .... and kissed when we met.

f And our .... on today's show is Robbie Williams.

g Are you happy with the money from your job,
   or do you want a ....?

h What's the .... in Hollywood this
   week? Who's leaving their husband or wife
   and who is marrying for a third time?

i Suddenly someone .... on our back door. Who was it?

GUESS WHAT

What happens after the end of the story? Choose from these ideas or add your own.

a Fay marries Wing.

b Fay leaves Studio Five.

c Fay and Jason are now friends again.

d Simon goes back to live with his mother.

e Simon goes to look for his real father in Australia.

f Wing makes a new show at Sun Radio.

g Jason comes back to Studio Five.

h ....

i ....

j ....

PROJECT A   *Cards and Special Days*

**1 What is happening to these different people? What do you say to them?
Match the words with the pictures.**

a Simon's got a new job.

b Mrs Jones is 51 today.

c Jason's feeling ill this week.

d Amy's mother died at the weekend.

1 Happy Birthday!

2 Get well soon!

3 I'm really sorry to hear about your mother.

4 Congratulations on your new job!

2 Match these cards with the words in them.

1 Congratulations to the two of you on your wedding day!

2 Congratulations on your retirement – after all these years!

3 Congratulations on passing your driving test!

4 Many happy returns of the day – Birthday Boy!

3 Complete this dialogue with the phrases from the box.

Amy: ....

Fay: ....

Amy: Here´s a card for you. Open it.

Fay opens the card.

Wing: ....

Fay: (*reading*) Congratulations from all of us at Sun Radio.

Wing: ....

Amy: ....

Fay opens the present.

Fay: .... Thank you, Amy.

And here´s a present from all of us, too.	Congratulations on your wedding day!	Oh, look! A beautiful clock and a wonderful key box.
Thank you very much, Amy.	That's very nice.	What does it say, Fay?

4 Match these characters from *Studio Five* with the best presents for them. Can you think of any more good presents for each character?

Jason	an all-Europe train ticket
Simon	an Italian love music CD
Mrs Jones	a keyring
Wing	a dog
Zoë	an expensive pen and pencil

5 Choose three characters from *Studio Five*, a special day, and some presents. Write a dialogue like the one in Activity 3.

PROJECT A *Going by Underground*

1 Fay went to visit Mrs Jones by underground. Look at the map and Fay's diary page. Mark Fay's route on the map like this: ⎯ ⎯ ⎯ ⎯ ⎯ ⎯ ⎯ .

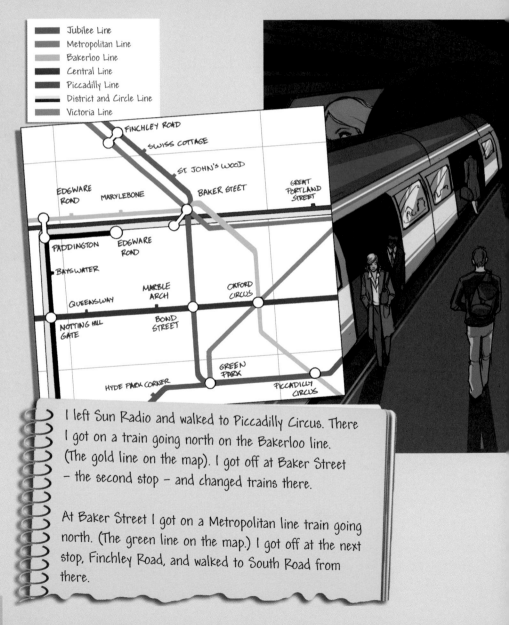

Jubilee Line
Metropolitan Line
Bakerloo Line
Central Line
Piccadilly Line
District and Circle Line
Victoria Line

FINCHLEY ROAD
SWISS COTTAGE
ST JOHN'S WOOD
EDGWARE ROAD
MARYLEBONE
BAKER STEET
GREAT PORTLAND STREET
PADDINGTON
EDGWARE ROAD
BAYSWATER
QUEENSWAY
MARBLE ARCH
OXFORD CIRCUS
NOTTING HILL GATE
BOND STREET
GREEN PARK
HYDE PARK CORNER
PICCADILLY CIRCUS

I left Sun Radio and walked to Piccadilly Circus. There I got on a train going north on the Bakerloo line. (The gold line on the map). I got off at Baker Street – the second stop – and changed trains there.

At Baker Street I got on a Metropolitan line train going north. (The green line on the map.) I got off at the next stop, Finchley Road, and walked to South Road from there.

2 Answer the questions.

   a How many underground lines did Fay take?

   b Which direction did she go in? (North, east, south or west?)

   c Where did she change lines?

   d How many stops was the last stop from the first station?

3 Look at the map and complete the diary page about Fay's journey from Sun Radio to Paddington Station.

I left Sun Radio quickly and walked at once to
(a).. . There I got on a train
going north on the (b)...................................... line.
(The (c)...................... line on the map). I got off
at Oxford Circus – the (d)............................... stop
– and changed trains there.

At Oxford Circus, I got on a (e)..................................
line train going west. (The (f)...................................
line on the map.) I got off at the (g)...........................
stop, Notting Hill Gate – and changed trains there.

At Notting Hill Gate, I got on a (h)...........................
and (i)...................................... line train
going north. (The (j)....................... and
(k)........................ lines on the map.) I got off at the
(l).................................... stop, Paddington – and I
walked up to the train station from there.

4 **Mrs Jones came from home to meet Fay at Sun Radio. Look at
the map on page 42 and her notes below. Answer these questions.**

   a How many underground lines did Mrs Jones take?

   b Which direction did she go in? (North, east, south or west?)

   c Where did she change lines?

   d How many stops was it from the first station?

> Finchley Road – Jubilee
> Line (south) – 5 stops
> – change Green Park –
> Piccadilly line (east) –
> 1 stop

5 **Write about Mrs Jones's journey. Use these phrases to help you.**

I left home .... I walked to
.... underground station.

There I got on a train going .... on the
.... line. (The .... line
on the map).

I got off at .... – the ....
stop (and changed trains there to the
.... line going ....).
I got off at .... – the ....
stop. I walked to .... from there.

GRAMMAR CHECK

need and need to

We use the verb need/don't need to talk about important things for us to have. Need is a regular verb.

Do you need more time, Fay?   *I don't need your help!*

We use need to/don't need to + infinitive without *to* to talk about important things for us to do.

We need to think of ideas for the show.   *You don't need to leave your flat, Simon.*

1 Complete the sentences with the correct past or present form of *need* or *need to*. Who do you think said these things? Write Fay, Wing, Mrs Jones, or Simon.

a 'I ...don't need. a card, but I'm looking for a friend.'   .....Fay.....

b 'Meet me in the coffee shop at 10 o'clock. We .... talk.'   ....

c 'For years I thought, "I .... tell Simon about his real dad".'   ....

d 'I .... my keys, but they're in my bag!'   ....

e 'I think we .... listen to the CD again, Fay.'   ....

f 'Excuse me. I .... my bag. A woman left it here last night.'   ....

g 'You .... help, Fay. I can stay here and think of ideas for the show.'

     ....

h 'Please help me to find my son. I .... you.'   ....

i 'You .... worry, Mr Khan. She isn't going to come back to your shop.'

     ....

j 'No, I .... more time to think of new ideas. Monday is OK for me.'

     ....

k 'I don't want to call Jason, but I .... get into the radio station.'

     ....

GRAMMAR CHECK

Past Simple: negative

To make the Past Simple negative, we use didn't + infinitive without *to* for most verbs.

Jason didn't run after me.

I didn't love Jason. I loved Wing.

2 **One piece of information in each sentence is incorrect. Change the word in italics and correct the sentences.**

a Fay and Wing listened to *music* in the studio at night.

...... *Fay and Wing didn't listen to music. They listened to* .... *the CD from the show.* ......

b Simon phoned the show from *an airport*.

....

c Fay went to a *bookshop*.

....

d Fay left her *phone* in the shop.

....

e A woman left Fay's bag at the *ticket* office.

....

f Fay went back to *Simon's mother's* house.

....

g Jason took Fay to *the cinema*.

....

h *Wing* tried to kiss Fay.

....

i A man put a *key* into her bag.

....

j Fay met *Wing* in a café.

....

k Simon and his *father* talked on Fay's show.

....

GRAMMAR CHECK

Past Simple: information questions

We use question words + did + subject + infinitive without *to* to make Past Simple questions for most verbs.

Why did he leave?   *When did you lose it?*

3 **Fay is interviewing Simon's mother on her show. Write Fay's questions using *what*, *why*, or *how*.**

a Simon's real father / do?

What did Simon's real father do?

b he / go / to Australia?

....

c Simon / learn about his real father?

....

d Simon / leave home?

....

e you / do?

....

f you / get / from Simon on your birthday?

....

g Simon / phone / my programme?

....

4 **Match these answers with Fay's questions in Exercise 3.**

1 He sent me some flowers. So he was OK, I knew. ☐

2 He was very angry with me because I didn't tell him about his real father. ☐

3 He wanted to tell me, 'I'm OK, Mum.' But I want him to come home! ☐

4 He left me when I was pregnant, and went to Australia. ⓐ

5 He read an old letter from his real father. ☐

6 I looked for him for months. I put photos in shops and called the police. Where was he? Nobody knew. ☐

7 He was selfish. I was pregnant and he didn't want a baby. ☐

Requests with can

We use Can I ... ? or Can we ... ? + infinitive without *to* to ask if we can do something.

Can I help you?   Can we go now?

We use Can you + infinitive without *to* to ask someone to do something.

Can you close your eyes for a minute?

We put a question mark (?) at the end of requests with *can*.

5 **Write these people's requests. Use the word in brackets.**

   a Wing wants Fay to answer one more call. (you)

      Wing: *'Can you answer one more call?'*

   b Fay wants to see Simon's room. (I)

      Fay: ....

   c Fay wants Khan to tell her about Simon. (you)

      Fay: ....

   d Fay wants to talk with Mrs Jones about Simon. (we)

      Fay: ....

   e Simon's mum wants Fay to help her. (you)

      Mrs Jones: ....

   f Fay wants to have a big coffee with milk. (I)

      Fay: ....

   g Fay wants Jason to open the door for her. (you)

      Fay: ....

   h Jason would like to be friends with Fay. (we)

      Jason: ....

   i Simon wants to meet Fay in the coffee shop. (we)

      Simon: ....

   j Jason wants to buy dinner for Fay. (I)

      Jason: ....

   k Fay wants Simon's mum to come to the radio station. (you)

      Fay: ....

GRAMMAR CHECK

Modal auxiliary verbs: could and couldn't

We use could/couldn't + infinitive without *to* to talk about past ability.

On the computer, we could hear them easily.

I opened my bag, but I couldn't find my keys in it.

6 **Complete these sentences. Use *could* or *couldn't* and one of the verbs in the box.**

find	get	get	get	go	hear
meet	move	talk	~~think~~		

a Fay .....couldn't think..... of any new ideas for her radio show.

b Wing and Fay .... the CD because it was in Jason's office and the door was locked.

c Fay .... into Jason's office after she walked along the window ledge.

d When Wing put the CD into the computer, they .... something about a train to Oxford.

e Fay went to Paddington Station, but she .... Simon at the card shop.

f She .... her bag from the lost property office because it was closed.

g She .... home because her keys were in her bag.

h Simon and Fay .... because Simon left a note in Fay's bag.

i After Jason moved up to Studio Ten, Fay .... into Jason's office.

j After Fay's show, Simon's mum .... to Simon and see him again.

Countable and uncountable nouns

We use many with countable nouns.

I went into the shop. It had many different things in it.

We use much with uncountable nouns in questions and negative sentences.

It was Friday and I didn't have much time.

We use a few with countable nouns and a little with uncountable nouns.

I wanted to ask him a few questions.   *We had a little wine.*

We use no and a lot of/lots of with countable and uncountable nouns.

I had no money and no keys to the Sun Radio offices.

He has a lot of shops in London.

7   **Choose the correct words to complete the conversation.**

Simon: Can you tell me something, Fay? How did you find me?

Fay: My friend Wing and I listened to a CD of your phone call a) **many/much** times.
         Where did you call from? We wanted to find out, but there wasn't b) **many/much** background noise on the CD. Then Wing played it on a computer. It was
         a really good idea.

Simon: Why?

Fay: We could hear c) **a lot of/a little** new sounds in the background. We heard
         you when you put d) **a little/a few** coins into the phone box.

Simon: But how e) **many/much** phone boxes are there in London?

Fay: I know, but we heard f) **a few/much** words about a train to Oxford, too.

Simon: So you looked at Oxford trains on the Internet and came to Paddington Station?

Fay: That's right. I visited g) **a few/a little** shops and took your picture with me.
         h) **Lots of/Much** people looked at it, but nobody knew you.

Simon: That's because my hair is different. And people here call me Jim.

Fay: Right. I was really worried by then because I had i) **no/a few** more ideas, and
         I didn't have j) **much/many** time to find you. And then you left me that note.

Simon: Well, you needed k) **a few/a little** help, I thought!

GRAMMAR

GRAMMAR CHECK

Present Continuous for future: affirmative and negative

We can use the Present Continuous to talk about a planned future arrangement.

We form the Present Continuous with the verb be + –ing.

⊕ *Jason's moving up to Studio Ten next month.*

⊖ *Wing isn't working with Fay next month.*

8 Look at Fay's diary and write affirmative and negative sentences about Fay's day.

Thursday 10th May	
08:00	
09:00	
10:00	10.00 coffee with Simon before show
11:00	11.00 –12.00 'Friends' Hour' interview with Simon
12:00	12.30 lunch with Amy
13:00	
14:00	14.00 studio meeting (3 hours)
15:00	
16:00	
17:00	17.30 wedding dress shop
18:00	
19:00	
20:00	20.00 dinner with Wing's parents at the Mexican restaurant

Contact New Event Actions View Options

a Fay / talk / to Mrs Jones on *The Friends' Hour*

....*Fay isn't talking to Mrs Jones on The Friends' Hour.*....

b Fay / meet / Simon for coffee at ten ....

c she / have / lunch with Jason at twelve thirty ....

d the people in the studio / have / a meeting at two ....

e she / go / home after work ....

f she / visit / a dress shop at five thirty ....

g she / meet / Wing's parents at eight ....

h they / eat / in a Chinese restaurant ....

DOMINOES
THE STRUCTURED APPROACH TO READING IN ENGLISH

Dominoes is an enjoyable series of illustrated classic and modern stories in four carefully graded language stages — from Starter to Three — which take learners from beginner to intermediate level.

Each *Domino* reader includes:
- a good story to read and enjoy
- integrated activities to develop reading skills and increase active vocabulary
- personalized projects to make the language and story themes more meaningful
- seven pages of grammar activities for consolidation.

Each *Domino* pack contains a reader, plus a MultiROM with:
- a complete audio recording of the story, fully dramatized to bring it to life
- interactive activities to offer further practice in reading and language skills and to consolidate learning.

If you liked this Level One *Domino*, why not read these?

Housemates
Alison Watts

Chris leaves his home in a small town in Australia to go and study at the University of Sydney. He needs to find somewhere to live.

But it's not easy to find a house to share in a big city. Every house has its problems, and not all of Chris's housemates are easy to live with. In fact, some of them are very difficult people!

Can Chris find the house that he needs with housemates that he can live with?

Book ISBN: 978 0 19 424764 1
MultiROM Pack ISBN: 978 0 19 424728 3

Macbeth
William Shakespeare

A dark, rainy day in Scotland, long ago. Returning from battle, Macbeth and his friend Banquo meet three witches. 'Macbeth, the king!' they say, but Macbeth is not a king, he is just a simple soldier.

Macbeth and Banquo cannot forget the witches' words. Soon Macbeth is king, but his wife walks in her sleep at night, and dreams of blood. What lies in the future for Banquo? And how many people must die before Scotland finds peace once more?

Book ISBN: 978 0 19 424756 6
MultiROM Pack ISBN: 978 0 19 424720 7

You can find details and a full list of books in the *Dominoes* catalogue and Oxford English Language Teaching Catalogue, and on the website: www.oup.com/elt

Teachers: see www.oup.com/elt for a full range of online support, or consult your local office.

	CEF	Cambridge Exams	IELTS	TOEFL iBT	TOEIC
Starter	A1	YLE Movers	–	–	–
Level 1	A1–A2	YLE Flyers/KET	3.0	–	–
Level 2	A2–B1	KET-PET	3.0-4.0	–	–
Level 3	B1	PET	4.0	57-86	550